BHIP® Neurocognitive Executive Functioning Workbook

Dr. Kim Burgess

To my three children – eldest Joel, followed by twins Claire and Kyle – who all bumped up my executive functioning by virtue of our very busy lives with children, dogs, full-time work, and running a household. Going through years of education and raising children definitely drives home the crucial reasons for these neurocognitive executive functions and skills!

Middle and high school students so often struggle to develop crucial executive function skills like self-regulation, working memory, organization, planning and prioritizing that they need to succeed. Based on her research and her extensive clinical experience with kids and parents, the author has developed this super practical, relevant, and much needed workbook. It is chock full of useful exercises, strategies, and tools!! This book will be an invaluable resource for families and professionals.

- *Dr. Laura Kenealy, Ph.D., ABPP-CN; Director of the Executive Function Clinic, Division of Neuropsychology, Children's National Hospital, Washington DC.*

xecutive Functioning is a relatively new term for a skills' set that ve acquire during a lifetime of managing everyday life ituations. Delays in executive function development can cause a ascade of negative impacts on the lives of our children for earning, school progress, challenges with peers, arguing at home nd poor self-esteem to name a few.

Dr. Burgess walks us through a step-by-step program to advise rofessionals and parents in helping children and teenagers to elp themselves. Through an interactive approach, Dr. Burgess xplains and guides us through managing attention, working nemory, time management and organization. She then offers us "power-up" to help with task initiation, response inhibition and motional control. All of these skills culminate in metacognition – n ability to self-assess, self-monitor and self-correct.

hank you Dr. Burgess for again breaking down a complex topic nto easily understood and incorporated techniques!

- *Dr. Caren Glassman, M.D., Board-Certified Pediatrician, Fellow of the American Academy of Pediatrics*

Even the most academically gifted students can benefit from thi workbook. By encouraging students to reflect not only on what they study but also on how they study, Dr. Burgess empowers students to engage in independent and purposeful learning that will last them a lifetime.

- *Nancy Shay, Montgomery County Public Schools Teacher o the Year, 2017-2018*

Contents

Acknowledgements v

Foreword.. vi

THE WHAT AND WHY OF EXECUTIVE FUNCTIONING

Definition, Purpose, and Who Benefits? 1

Executive Functions and Skills.. 2

SELF-ASSESSMENT OF EXECUTIVE SKILLS 4

SUSTAINED ATTENTION

Definition and Recommendations to Improve It 11

What does your current study environment look like?............................ 13

WHERE you do homework is just as important as DOING your homework 15

In the classroom in-person pointers.. 16

Paying attention in class...17

I. WORKING MEMORY

Definition, Purpose, and Applying it.. 18

Tips for a School Morning Routine 19

II.TIME MANAGEMENT AND PRIORITIZING

Managing Your Time 20

Time Wasters versus Time Users.. 21

More Reasons for Time Management and Prioritizing............................ 2

Keeping your Big Picture Priorities in Perspective 2

Why do I need to time manage and prioritize? 2

    Why Should I Care ...? 2

MONTHLY PLANNER... 3

    Make your own Monthly Planner 3

WEEKLY PLANNER/AGENDA BOOK 3

    Sample weekly planner 3

    Make your own Weekly Planner... 3

Long-term Projects.. 4

    Learning Balance: Make a pie chart! 4

IV. ORGANIZATION

Problems with Organization and their Solutions 4

Organizational Tools 4

    Use different apps/websites to make your life easier 5

How do you like to organize your notes?.................................... 5

    How to take good notes 5

V. TASK INITIATION

What "Doing your Homework" actually means: a 3-Step Process 5

Procrastinating in Situations, Self-Assessing Reasons, and Taking Action 5

The Cycle of Procrastination 6

Determine the steps for these tasks 6

Sequential Steps for Writing Assignments or Long-Term Assignments 67

  How to "chunk" writing assignments 68

How to focus when you don't want to do your homework 69

I. RESPONSE INHIBITION

Definition and Why it Matters 70

Self-Reflection and What To Do 70

  How to Have More Self-Control 71

II. EMOTIONAL CONTROL

What is it and Exercises to improve it 70

  Extra Pointer 76

  Take Heart and Remember 76

III. METACOGNITION

Definition, Self-Awareness, and How to Improve 77

Bonus Sections – Helping you Function Beyond Executive Function

Studying for Tests, Quizzes, and Exams 80

Helpful Study Habits 81

Sample Study Sheet 82

More Study Tips 83

Test-Taking Habits 84

  Use your Classmates to your and their Advantage 85

When You Feel Like You've Messed Up, What Do You Do? 86

Yet More Ways to Get Good Grades... 8

   What do you do about "bad" grades?... 9

   Whatever happens, cheating is never worth it............................. 9

Extra Information on Getting Along Well with Teachers 9

Final Considerations.. 9

Selected References... 9

Acknowledgements

Firstly, this book is dedicated to all the students, parents, teachers, and coaches from schools nationally and internationally who have been involved in the BHIP® Programs (www.bhipmethod.com). BHIP stands for "Biopsychosocial Health Intervention and Prevention" Programs. For invaluable contributions to BHIP, I thank Claire Wilson, Sally Simpson, Matthew Chazin, Kyle Wilson and Joel Wilson.

Secondly, Dr. Burgess would like to thank her scientific research collaborators – Professor Julie Bowker (SUNY-Buffalo) and Professor Paul Hastings (UC-Davis Mind & Brain Institute), as well as Miriam Stotsky (SUNY-Buffalo). Our research projects on preventions/ interventions for middle school and high school students have shown significant scientific evidence for their effectiveness in normative community samples (APA, 2020). This book is built upon BHIP's crucial developmental foundations and functioning of children and adolescents up to college age.

Thirdly, this book is dedicated to the Potomac Pediatrics practice in Rockville, Maryland, USA headed by the brilliant pediatrician Dr. Caren Glassman and her talented partners Jenna Vallejo and Dr. Amy Kaplan. They have been incredibly supportive from the beginnings of Dr. Burgess' BHIP Programs, as well as gave helpful input and resources that contributed to their overall success.

Foreword

Executive functioning underrides our abilities to go through daily life events, tasks, and running things in a smooth, efficient, and organized rather than haphazard manner. It affects everything from getting ready in the mornings to start your day to driving directions to follow through on projects or events.

Particularly during covid-19 time, kids are struggling with online learning and adults are stressed by too many 'zoom' meetings; yet our brains' cognitive skills can help us through responsibilities – and for that matter, general life! This book may lessen our stressors and struggles by providing assistance and answers for "What do we do about it?". Guidance for organizing our academic work and other life areas will be provided, prefaced by suggesting ways to self-assess your strengths and weaknesses in order to decide if or what you want to change. Then I provide pointers, tools, and advice for how to do it. Boosting executive functioning makes daily life less stressful!!

THE WHAT AND WHY OF EXECUTIVE FUNCTIONING

Definition, Purpose, and Who Benefits?

Executive functioning (EF) refers to higher order neurocognitive abilities that the frontal lobe of the brain manages. Some of these abilities are sustained attention, working memory, space and time organization, self-regulation, impulse control, cognitive flexibility, and others. Respectively, executive skills and function teach you *how and when* to manage various brain capacities.

There are many areas of functioning that EF skills are important for – learning, carrying out tasks/ jobs, academics, social interactions, and general functioning. Therefore, EF strengths are beneficial in important ways; conversely, EF weaknesses can compromise daily life skills and are often part of childhood dysfunction or disorders, such as ADHD/ADD, emotion/mood dysregulation, autism spectrum, or learning/ reading disabilities.

Not only does executive functioning cut across many psychological disorders and can be utilized for a range of kids' challenges, but also EF training benefits all the normative population to improve and optimize self-control, self-awareness, attentional, organizational, and time management abilities.

1

Executive Functions and Skills:

I. Sustained Attention – maintain focus, not easily distracted, concentration despite distractions; not mental fatigue or boredom

II. Working Memory – remembering information during complex tasks; sequence and carry out multiple steps

III. Time Management and Prioritizing – allocation and awareness of time; the ability to understand how to use time to your advantage; doing what's most important first

IV. Organization – creating a system to keep track of information; keep things uncluttered, not messy

V. Task Initiation - how to get started on a task without procrastination

VI. Response Inhibition – think before you act; opposite of impulsive

VII. Emotional Control – not getting easily frustrated, impatient, or anxious

VIII. Metacognition – reflecting; self-awareness, self-monitoring, self-assessing; being objective

SELF-ASSESSMENT OF EXECUTIVE SKILLS

1 = Rarely	2 = Sometimes	3 = Often

1. I don't plan ahead for assignments	
2. I study for tests the day before or the day of tests	
3. It's hard for me to prioritize my work or activities (which homework assignment or activity to do first)	
4. It's hard to break up long-term projects into smaller tasks and complete them	

SUM: _____

5. I'm often told that my schoolwork is messy	
6. I have trouble finding my stuff – like books, pens and pencils, shoes/boots, keys, assignments, or my jacket/coat	
7. I have trouble organizing things (my schoolwork, my desk, my room)	
8. I'll finish my homework, but then forget to hand it in	

SUM: _____

9. When I have a list of things to do, I remember 1 or 2 things, but not the rest	
10. It's hard to do tasks that have more than one step	
11. When I'm taught something, I forget it easily (sports or classroom teachings)	
12. When I re-read notes I wrote in class, I don't remember writing any of it	

SUM: _____

13. I get frustrated or angry pretty easily	
14. I have trouble controlling my emotions	
15. I get overwhelmed easily	
16. I get bothered or upset by things I forget about the day after	

SUM: _____

17. I tend to say or do things quickly rather than thinking them through	
18. I make careless mistakes	
19. It's hard waiting my turn (waiting in line, waiting for coach to play me)	
20. I'm often told that I'm interrupting people when they're talking	

SUM: _____

21. I have trouble paying attention	
22. I get distracted easily	
23. It's hard to follow through on things (like finishing schoolwork, projects, tasks, or chores)	
24. When I'm doing a task or writing something, I find it hard to stay on-task as long as other people can	

SUM: _____

6

1 = Rarely	2 = Sometimes	3 = Often

25. When someone suggests how to solve a problem that's different from my way, I usually stick with my own way	
26. I tend to get stuck on one task or activity and have trouble when I have to stop and move onto something else	
27. I don't like it when things change - like what I eat or when I have to break from my routine	
28. I don't like when my parents or my friends change plans from what we were going to do	

SUM: _____

29. My awareness of my own behavior isn't as good as it should be	
30. It's hard to know what my own strengths and weaknesses are	
31. It's hard to know when what I say or do bothers others.	
32. It's hard for me to decide whether something in class is important enough to write down, *or* I end up writing down too many details	

SUM: _____

1 = Rarely	2 = Sometimes	3 = Often

33.	I have trouble getting started on tasks, assignments, or projects	
34.	I am told that I procrastinate; told that I delay or take too long doing things; that I'm late for things	
35.	The stress of approaching deadlines makes it difficult for me to start tasks, assignments, or projects	
36.	When I'm starting something new, I can't figure out where to start	

SUM: _____

37.	It's hard for me to do work around my other commitments, like practices or family time	
38.	It's hard for me to estimate how long it will take me to complete a task	
39.	I spend a lot of time on one task or assignment, but don't have a lot of time to complete the rest of my tasks or assignments	
40.	It takes me longer than other people to get my schoolwork done	

SUM: _____

STATEMENTS	EXECUTIVE SKILLS	SUM
1-4	Planning/Prioritizing	
5-8	Organization	
9-12	Working Memory	
13-16	Emotional Control	
17-20	Response Inhibition	
21-24	Sustained Attention	
25-28	Flexibility	
29-32	Metacognition	
33-36	Task Initiation	
37-40	Time Management	

Stronger EF Skills (list skills with lower scores)	EF Skills Needing Improvement (list skills with higher scores)
1.	1.
2.	2.
3.	3.

Burgess & Simpson, 20:

Write about strengths **and** weaknesses:

_____

_____

_____

_____

From your scores, you now have a fairly good idea of your strengths and weaknesses. You're going to go through these sections to follow, but you might spend more time on the sections you found yourself needing to improve.

I.   SUSTAINED ATTENTION

Definition and Recommendations to Improve It

Just as it implies, sustained attention constitutes the ability to focus or concentrate on an activity, stimulus or task for a period of time long enough to finish, even when distractions are present. When doing in-person or online/distance or virtual learning and any work at home or elsewhere, here are some recommendations:

 Keep distractions to a minimum; and remove all irrelevant items around you

 Use apps to prevent access to distracting websites (Mac SelfControl, Anti-Social)

 Estimate time it takes to do tasks or activities; build in breaks to reduce mental fatigue

 Do work at school or another place before going home

Use apps to help re-focus attention (Interval Minder, Insight Timer)

 Do not multi-task

 Take breaks by exercising, which will re-invigorate your energy and focus

 Block yourself from using media while doing homework

What does your current study environment look like?

Location	□ Your bed
	□ In your room
	□ Your kitchen table
	□ The library
	□ A coffeeshop
	□ Your friend's house
Time of Day	□ In the morning before school
	□ During the school day
	□ Right after school
	□ After dinner
	□ When you should be sleeping (past 10 PM)
	□ Multiple times throughout the day
Sound	□ With music
	□ With TV in the background
	□ In total quiet
Alone or with others?	□ Alone
	□ In a group

Your brain cannot think clearly if it's surrounded by mess!.

WHERE you do homework is just as important as DOING your homework:

- Pick a location in your house that is free of distractions.
- How much work are you going to get done ...?

    o In the kitchen with the rest of your family?

    o While watching TV or Netflix?

    o In a messy room?

    o Surrounded by video games, phones, or other distractions?

- Doing homework in a quiet room of your house that is comfortable allows you to get MORE WORK DONE & FASTER.
- Use a table or desk you can write on and spread out all of your notes.
- Listen to music **if** that helps you focus and be more productive!

In the classroom in-person pointers:

Take notes

Sit near or at the front; make eye contact with the speaker

Participate in discussion and ask questions

Use self-talk to keep self on task: what should I be doing now?

Paying attention in class

It can be really hard to pay attention in class when you don't care what the teacher is saying, or it's the last class of the day, or it's a Friday and you're just tired and want to go home. ***Stay engaged with some of these tips:***

- o *Stay active by taking notes* – one way of paying attention since you're actively listening

- o *Sit near the front of the class* – helpful since the teacher is louder, the board is easier to see, and you're less likely to fall asleep or zone out when the teacher can easily see you

- o *Remind yourself why paying attention is important* – if you don't listen to what the teacher is saying and take notes on it, how are you going to remember it and study it for the test?

- o *Try not to talk in class when you're not supposed to* – it will only distract you, your classmates, and your teacher (btw, teachers can't stand this, and it makes you unpopular with them!)

II.   WORKING MEMORY

Definition, Purpose, and Applying it

Working memory entails short-term memory ability to temporarily store, process and manage information in order to d complex verbal and visual/spatial tasks. Whether we retain in our brain elements needed to carry out a task, *or* remember and respond during a conversation, affects many things.

We need working memory for learning, especially reading comprehension, reasoning, and mental operations involving sequencing. Break up instructions and tasks into smaller units; otherwise, you may experience brain overload!

Take getting ready for school in the mornings, for example:

How do you break that down into steps in order to remember everything to do and be on time for school?

_____

_____

_____

_____

Tips for a School Morning Routine:

Try doing the Upstairs/ Downstairs Morning Mode:

Chunk upstairs and ensure no need to go back upstairs again by doing these things first before going downstairs – bathroom, get dressed, make bed. Then, after ensuring all upstairs-related things are done, go downstairs – eat breakfast and brush teeth in downstairs bathroom. Put homework ready to turn in and lunch made the night before into your backpack.

As another example, take *writing an essay*. Which sequential steps would be helpful to break it down?

_____

_____

_____

_____

See page 67 in section V. Task Initiation under sequential steps for writing assignments or long-term assignments for a laid-out example of doing writing assignments.

III.TIME MANAGEMENT AND PRIORITIZING

Organizing your life, getting things done on time, and knowing how to order those things in terms of importance are life skills.

Managing Your Time

Develop	Develop a daily schedule including classes, sports, and recreational activity; allot a block of time for doing homework
Use	Use an agenda book, planner, or apps like Google Calendar
Prioritize	Prioritize (homework vs clubs, math homework vs social studies)
Think ahead	Think ahead based on your schedule as soon as you get assignments
Plan	Plan high school career too (classes, sports, and clubs)
Communicate	If your schedule is particularly difficult, communicate with your teachers
Don't count on	Don't count on teachers to remind you about long-term assignments
Take	Take advantage of social opportunities you do have

Time Wasters versus Time Users

"Time Wasters" usurp time and don't help you do what needs to be done. "Time Users" allow you to get things done. Place a check next to any of the activities that you engage in often and add any other activities that you may do on a regular basis. Some activities can be either "Time Wasters" or "Time Users" depending on how you use them.

For the following time wasters and time users, put a check in the boxes that apply to you. Next, list 2-3 other time wasters and time users that apply to you in the remaining spaces of the table.

Time Wasters	*Time Users*
□ Watching TV	□ Completing homework
□ Playing video games	□ Practicing your instrument
□ Texting	□ Studying for a test
□ Surfing the Internet	□ Cleaning the house
□ Talking on the phone	□ Finishing a craft project

☐ Being on Social Media (Snapchat, Instagram, YouTube, etc.)	☐ Playing your sport outside

Prioritizing means determining which activities are important and need your immediate attention and which activities are less important, but still need to be done.

Prioritize your activities by rating them as 1=low importance, 2=medium importance, or 3=high importance:

Study for a test:	_____	Text K:	_____	Stop in office to get pass:	_____
Get ready for school:	_____	Eat dinner:	_____	Go to bed on time:	_____
Play video games:	_____	Catch the bus:	_____	Eat breakfast:	_____

Now, make a list of the activities you do during a typical day and prioritize them in the same way:

How would you prioritize different assignments within the homework you need to get done?

_____

_____

_____

_____

_____

Reflect on the following statements and rate how often (seldom, sometimes, often) they apply to you:

	How much? seldom, sometimes, or often
Do you start with the homework that is most pressing (the stuff that's due tomorrow)?	
Do you do the "easier" stuff first: Fill-in-the-blank worksheets, assignments from classes that you like, anything that takes minimal effort/brainpower?	
Do you put your full effort into the more difficult stuff (like assignments from classes you don't like)?	
Do you get frustrated and give up if you can't figure something out?	

If you find yourself seldom starting homework until it's getting late, or you're often getting frustrated, recognize it's difficult to prioritize your work in these ways. On the other hand, even if you're not getting frustrated or feeling burdened, the pointers below are relevant and helpful.

More Reasons for Time Management and Prioritizing:

- Always remember how you feel about getting homework done. Do you feel relieved, proud, or accomplished? Noticing that might motivate you even more the next time.

- Time managing and prioritizing help you get you in the zone for doing more work.

- Prioritizing helps you get the 'less liked' work out of the way and you spend less time on it!

- If you can't figure something out, DON'T GIVE UP OR GET FRUSTRATED. Take a break and come back to it. If you still can't figure it out, ask a parent, sibling, classmate, or your teacher for help! Try to solve problems in a different way.

eeping your Big Picture Priorities in Perspective

Vhen you're figuring out what classes and other volunteer
ctivities to do, it can be overwhelming with all the options
vailable. Keep yourself grounded by starting from your end goal
nd working backwards to realize what is *really* important to you.

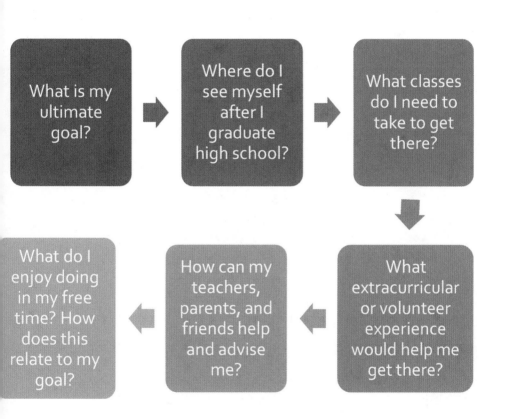

Why do I need to time manage and prioritize?

By setting aside time blocks specifically for homework and other responsibilities you...:

Don't have to be stressed by rushing to complete homework or chores at the last minute	Did you realize this? Circle one:	Knew this already
		Didn't know this
Won't be in class unprepared (not having your homework, not being prepared to answer questions from the teacher, not ready for a quiz/test)	Did you realize this? Circle one:	Knew this already
		Didn't know this
Don't have to miss out on hanging out with your friends or other fun activities because you didn't do your homework/chores	Did you realize this? Circle one:	Knew this already
		Didn't know this
Don't have to worry about your parents annoying you every 5 seconds to do something	Did you realize this? Circle one:	Knew this already
		Didn't know this

Why Should I Care ...?

You may have good time management skills now, but your schedule is only going to get more complicated and you're only going to have more responsibilities later on in high school and beyond. Starting these habits now are so much easier than trying to break the bad habit of procrastination later. Lots of college students often procrastinate, which gives them a tougher time.

If you give yourself enough time to fully complete an assignment to the best of your ability, you're not going to be rushing to complete it and possibly make careless mistakes	Did you realize this? Circle one:	Knew this already Didn't know this
You can avoid all the stress from rushing or realizing you don't have something to turn in	Did you realize this? Circle one:	Knew this already Didn't know this

Starting homework ASAP gives you more free time for the rest of the day to whatever you want and more time for SLEEP	Did you realize this? Circle one: Knew this already Didn't know this
Learn good habits NOW instead of having to break bad habits later when homework is harder and grades matter even more	Did you realize this? Circle one: Knew this already Didn't know this
Study and work habits that you start now are going to be with you for the rest of your life	Did you realize this? Circle one: Knew this already Didn't know this

MONTHLY PLANNER

- Use a monthly calendar for setting goals (and rewarding yourself). For example, by March 5th I want to complete my Social Studies project and then I will reward myself with free time!

- Write down major assignments, assessments, and school events

- Make note of important monthly events like friends' birthdays, holidays, events your friends are participating in, and more.

- While you can also include your daily activities like practices or your school schedule in your monthly planner, it's best to be able to visualize all the bigger stuff coming up without the clutter of daily events.

Today < > March 2021

Q ⌾ ⚙ Month ▾ ⸬

SUN	MON	TUE	WED	THU	FRI	SAT
28	Mar 1	2	3 Dylan's Birthday	4	5 Start Social Studies Project	6 Soccer Game
7	8 Permission Slip Due	9	10	11	12 Museum Field Trip	13
14 Soccer Game	15	16	17 History Report Due	18	19 Emily's Play	20 Soccer Game
21	22 English Essay Due	23	24	25 Violin Recital	26 Math Unit Test	27
28 Soccer Game	29	30	31	Apr 1	2	3

Make your own Monthly Planner

What does the typical month look like for you?

Make sure to fill in the following:

- Major school assignments (essays, long-term projects)

- Upcoming tests

- Events for your extracurriculars (games, recitals, performances)

- Field trips

- Friends' birthdays

- Any necessary steps you need to complete any of these events (get field trip permission slip signed, start history report, study, etc.)

SUN	MON	TUE	WED	THU	FRI	SAT
28	Mar 1	2	3	4	5	6
7	8	9	10	11	12	13
14	15	16	17	18	19	20
21	22	23	24	25	26	27
28	29	30	31	Apr 1	2	3

WEEKLY PLANNER/AGENDA BOOK

More classes per day and more independence means that middle and high schoolers are responsible for their own schedule.

- Write your schedule with the teacher's name and location of the classroom in an easily accessible place in your agenda book. That way you'll know exactly where you have to go and you can avoid being late for class.

- Write down any assignments for each class with their due dates and check your agenda book before going to bed. Don't assume you'll remember everything!

- Personalize your agenda books with color-coding, different color pens/markers, and post-it notes to make staying organized more fun!

- Physically crossing something off your to-do list makes you feel accomplished

Use a weekly calendar for blocking off time to do homework.

- e.g., I will do my reading assignment after school from 3-5 before soccer practice

Sample weekly planner:

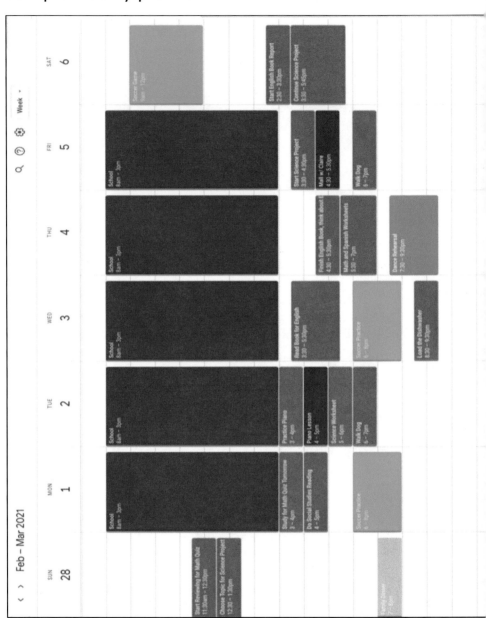

Make your own Weekly Planner

Start with things that are set in stone (school, family dinner, sports' games, practices/rehearsals). This way allows you to visualize the specific time blocks you have throughout the day that are *free.*

Then set aside specific blocks of time for you to do your homework, chores, and other responsibilities before planning social time.

How would you make time for HW and chores?

_____

_____

_____

_____

_____

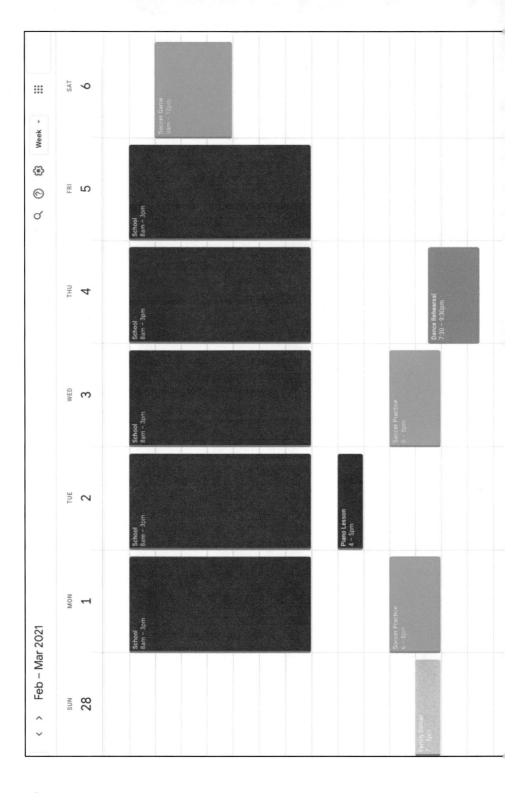

38

How would you rate your ability to manage your time on a scale of 1-5? (1 = poor; 5 = great): _____

Write a story about when you missed the bus and were late for school:

_____

_____

_____

_____

_____

Write about a time you *didn't* study for a test you had:

_____

_____

_____

_____

_____

Write about a time when you *didn't* finish your homework and maybe lied when asked about it:

_____

_____

_____

_____

_____

Long-term Projects

- Avoid doing all the work for a long-term project the night before it's due by giving yourself daily or weekly assignments or tasks to accomplish

- Example Tips: on Monday you might do research and take notes; on Wednesday you'll look for pictures to add to your presentation and do a bibliography; then on Friday you'll compile the power point and give yourself a weekend to prepare before the project is due the next Monday!

Learning Balance: Make a pie chart!

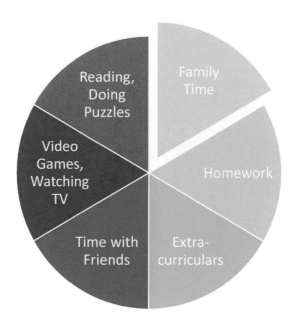

Think about all the time that you have per week. Make a pie char

showing how you think your free time SHOULD be divided up:

Now make a pie chart showing how your free time ACTUALLY IS divided up:

IV. ORGANIZATION

Organization is being able to keep things you need where they can be found quickly so that you will be more efficient in daily activities. Moreover, organization affects many aspects of our lives.

If our rooms, backpacks, folders, and lockers are disorganized, then our lives and what's going on in our brains probably are too Nothing feels worse than coming home from a tough day at school to an unmade bed with clothes all over the floor, or not being able to find homework in your backpack that you KNOW you did. You may feel like you don't have enough time for cleaning your room, but a cluttered room is only going to make you feel more stressed.

- Start the day by making your bed. As you're getting ready don't leave clothes on the floor and let them pile up. If you're not wearing them, then put them back in your drawer/closet.

- Have folders for each one of your classes. This allows you to have a specific place where you keep papers, notes, and anything else for every class. Have a section of your notebook for every classes' notes.

- Everything is in one place, so you don't have to search for a specific paper.

- As you are working, keep your desk clean and organized.

Problems with Organization and their Solutions

Losing things

> *Solution:* use folders only, backpack, check your area, always put back in same place

Forgetting to do or to bring something

> *Solution:* Use Reminders app, calendar or planner. When you think of or remember something, do it right away!

Forgetting an event

> *Solution:* Use Google Calendar, school planner

List of disorganized behavior DJ chose	How this behavior affects DJ
Did not have his homework in his backpack	(1) Had to scramble to catch the bus (2) Lower grades
Stuffed the paper into his backpack	(1) May not be able to find it later (2) It will get all wrinkled
Ran out the door to the bus	(1) Forgot his lunch
Couldn't find his math homework	(1) Lower grade
Did not write down that he had a science test	(1) Didn't study (2) Lower grade
Dropped his belongings on the floor when he got home	(1) Might not be able to find them later
Played video games and watched TV when he got home from school. Told his mom he had no homework	(1) Won't study for science test, won't find his math homework, etc.

Disorganized behavior in my life	How this behavior affects me
Ex. messy backpack	Can't find my homework assignments so I get lower grades

Organizational Tools

Put a check in the left column next to the one(s) that you already use and a minus sign if you don't. Add 2-3 more that may have been missed. Consider incorporating into your life the ones with a minus sign.

	Sticky notes
	To-do lists
	Desk organizer (trays or containers for organizing school supplies)
	Paper or electronic calendar
	"Landing spot" or "Take-off pad" – put in a basket or another container your important stuff as soon as you walk in the door (to develop habits)
	Apps – *Remember the Milk, Evernote, Google Keep*
	Backpack checklist
	Agenda book or planner

Use different apps/websites to make your life easier:

Quizlet – Flashcard App
- Sometimes easier to type flashcards than write them
- Has different game/activities for learning
- Great for learning vocab for different languages

Noodle Tools for writing
Teachers love assigning homework on this
Helpful for keeping track of sources, quotes, notes, and citations for research
Helpful for organizing your ideas and starting the writing process

Zotero
- Helpful for collecting, organizing, and citing your research
- Similar to EasyBib

Flora – Focus Habit Tracker App
- Set a timer to stay off your phone and plant a tree; if you can't put down your phone the tree dies
- Great app for self-control

he studying and note-taking habits you start now will serve you
ell throughout the rest of your life!

- Good study and homework habits are essential to success in middle school, high school, and college.

- It is better to start good habits now than to break bad habits later in your school career.

- Don't wait until you receive bad grades before you break bad habits – intentionally start to practice good habits.

- Staying organized and keeping an agenda book and calendar have helped countless college students manage their workload.

How do you like to organize your notes?

Handwritten or Typed?	☐ Handwritten ☐ Typed
Format (how is information organized?)	☐ Outline ☐ Like my teacher's power points ☐ Info separated by main ideas ☐ Use bullet points or indentations without a rea organizational system ☐ I write down whatever, wherever
How much stuff do you write down?	☐ I don't really write anything down, I just listen ☐ I write down all my teacher's main points, but I don't really write down many details ☐ I try to write down the most important information from the slides in my own words ☐ I write down every single word my teacher says
Do you rewrite or review your notes?	☐ I write down notes in class and never look at them again ☐ I only look over my notes before tests and quizzes ☐ I make a study sheet/rewrite some notes before tests and quizzes ☐ I rewrite every note multiple times until I get it

There are various ways to write notes in class - the most important things are that you have a consistent system that works for you *and* that you are engaging with the material in an active way. While taking notes by itself is active, you should also be engaging with the material further than writing things down word-for-word.

Which consistent system have you found works for you?

_____

_____

_____

Are there some note-taking styles that work better for different school subjects (such as English and History versus Math)?

_____

_____

_____

If you haven't found a consistent system, which methods would you like to try incorporating?

_____

_____

_____

_____

_____

_____

ow to take good notes:

- Everyone develops their own note-taking style based on how they learn and retain information.

- Take notes in a way that makes sense to you. Some may find it easy to organize things into an outline, bullet points, main ideas, etc.

- Teachers put information on slides for a reason – if it's on a slide, it's important enough to copy down! Slides can also be a good template for how to organize your notes.

- Keep your notes neat because it's important that you're able to read them while studying! If you need to write quickly, it might be helpful to rewrite your notes later.

- Use highlighters, different fonts, different colored pens/markers to personalize your notes.

- Being able to take good notes will help you in high school and college so start good habits now!

V.   TASK INITIATION

Knowing how and where to start an activity, or start anything for that matter, can be a challenge sometimes, especially if it is complicated.

What "Doing your Homework" actually means: a 3-Step Process

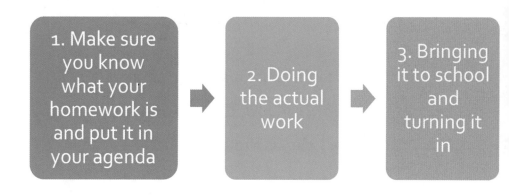

Procrastinating in Situations, Self-Assessing Reasons, and Taking Action

What does "procrastination" mean?

_____

_____

_____

_____

_____

What are some of the reasons why you procrastinate? Put a check in the column that applies to you for each of the following reasons for procrastinating. Next, add 2-3 more of your own:

Reasons for procrastinating	How much does it interfere with you being able to get it done		
	1 – not at all	2 – somewhat	3 – a lot
Don't know how to start the task			
Afraid you'll fail or be seen as incapable			

The task is boring, and you have trouble keeping your attention			

Think about the specific tasks you procrastinate on and list them in column 1. In column 2, write why you think you avoid each task.

Task being avoided	Reason for avoiding it
Ex. Starting my history paper	I haven't done the reading; I don't know where to start; I hate my history teacher; I still have 3 days left
Ex. Making my bed	I'm late for school and don't have time. Who cares anyway? Nobody is going to see it.

Think of a time you chose to procrastinate...

- What was the situation?

  _____

  _____

  _____

- Why did you avoid it?

  _____

  _____

  _____

- What problems did this create for you?

  _____

  _____

  _____

Think of a time you chose *not* to procrastinate...

- What was the situation?

  _____

  _____

  _____

- Why didn't you avoid it?

  _____

  _____

  _____

- What problems did you avoid by doing this?

  _____

  _____

  _____

Which situation went better?

_____

How might you change situations (like the first one) to help you procrastinate less in the future?

_____

_____

_____

_____

_____

The Cycle of Procrastination

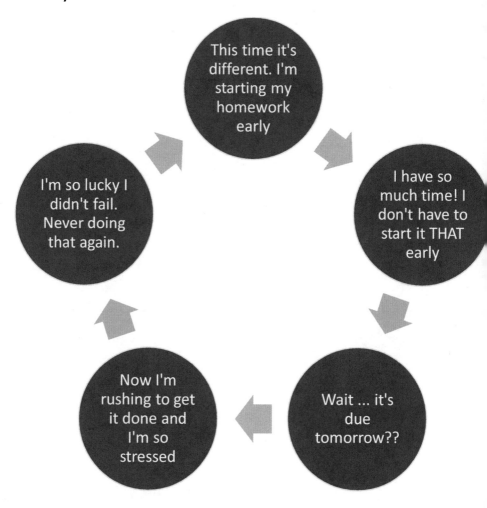

Break down tasks and projects into different steps to make larger tasks more manageable

Determine the steps for these tasks:

Task	Step 1: first thing you *do* to start the task	Step 2: the main task	Step 3: how you *know* the task is finished
Washing the dishes	Rinse gunk and food off	Clean with soap and sponge, rinse	Dry and put away
Walking the dog			
Cleaning your room			
Doing a puzzle			
Writing a book report			

Completing a writing assignment			

Sequential Steps for Writing Assignments or Long-term Assignments:

1 Book report due on April 4th, 2021

2 Note the due date. See how long you have to complete it.

3 Break down the work. Use notecards to help you write down every task the assignment involves. Be as specific as possible to help you stay on task.

4 Assign a due date for each step and mark it on the calendar. Use color-coding to help visualize the length of time you have for each task or use your project planner.

5 Have someone check in on your progress regularly (or check in with the teacher) and revise plan as needed.

How to "chunk" writing assignments:

1. REVIEW TYPE OF WRITING – Research? Personal story? Analysis of reading?

2. LIST TASKS AND CREATE TIMELINE – gather info, do research and/or read, take notes, decide on thesis statement, create an outline, write first draft, revise, review.

3. GATHER RESOURCES

4. READ & HIGHLIGHT INFORMATION

5. DECIDE ON A THESIS STATEMENT– determine the argument or main point.

6. CREATE AN OUTLINE/REVIEW PARAGRAPHS NEEDED – use a graphic organizer or note cards.

7. WRITE THE DRAFT

8. REVIEW, REVISE, AND RE-READ

How to focus when you don't want to do your homework:

- Putting off work that you don't want to do by procrastinating or distracting yourself will only make the work take up more of your time and cause yourself more problems in the long run.

- Avoid a bad grade, your parents constantly telling you to do your homework, missing out on extracurriculars or hanging out with friends, and losing sleep.

- Set small goals for yourself (like finishing your introductory paragraph or complete 5 math problems) and allow yourself breaks/rewards.

Getting your homework done ahead of time means you have more time to hang out with friends/family, more time for extracurriculars, more free time, more sleep, and overall less stress about homework!

VI. RESPONSE INHIBITION

Definition and Why it Matters:

Response inhibition is the ability to stop and think through befor taking too quick an action – impulse control. Responding too quickly means distractors get in our way, or the 'oops' behaviors that happen too often when we should have slowed down and implemented a decision process versus a fast reaction that leads to trouble.

Self-Reflection and What To Do:

Try 'response inhibition' exercises such as taking one primary tas (e.g., cleaning up your room) while making oneself block out distractors (e.g., looking at your phone).

How does this compare to focusing on a distractor when you're trying to complete the initial primary task?

_____

_____

_____

Reflect on the following statements and rate how often (seldom, sometimes, often) they apply to you:

	How much? seldom, sometimes, or often
Do you interrupt your teachers and get called out for it?	
Do you find yourself saying something you regret later?	
Do you ever do quick actions (like grab or hit ppl) that accidentally end up hurting them?	
Do you make careless errors on tests/exams because you rushed and didn't think it through?	

How to Have More Self-Control

Red Light/ Green Light Method: Visualize a red light or stop sign with your impulsive actions (e.g., interrupting in class, careless mistakes, physical actions).

Count to 5 Method: A stop-gap for acting impulsively is counting to 5 before reacting in ways that don't work for you.

VII. EMOTIONAL CONTROL

What is it and Exercises to improve it:

Emotional control is your ability to handle distress, tolerate upset, and distract yourself until the emotions subside. Coping through frustration, impatience, anger, disappointment or sadness is a tall order at times.

- Do an activity that requires concentration – what would be a good example for you?

  _____

  _____

  _____

- Focus on someone or something other than yourself – who or what would that be for you?

  _____

  _____

  _____

Compare yourself to other tough times – what other tough times have you experienced?

_____

_____

_____

Do something that creates the opposite feelings – what would that be for you?

_____

_____

_____

Push negative thoughts out of your mind for later – how could you do that?

_____

_____

_____

- Think about something else, think of one thing at a time – what else could you think about?

_____

_____

_____

- Bring sensations to life – think of a thing for each sense and how you can apply it?

_____

_____

_____

Vision

- Notice what is around you and see the details

Sound

- Listen to sounds that comfort

Smell

- Perfume/cologne, clean laundry, incense, baking

Taste

- Mindfully have a small treat

Touch

- Pet your animal, get under a soft blanket, massage, warm bath

Extra Pointer:

 Challenge yourself = decrease suffering by accepting discomfort rather than fighting it; use your resources to move forward

Take Heart and Remember:

 Accepting it is not liking it, approving it, or giving in

VIII. METACOGNITION

Definition, Self-Awareness, and How to Improve

Literally, metacognition translates into "thinking about thinking". It is the ability to self-reflect on one's thoughts, actions, plan of actions (strategies). It is *knowing how you know*.

One big way to boost your metacognitive ability is to use "self-talk". This causes us to rise above what we're naturally doing to reflect on what we're doing and how.

Professional athletes who work with sports psychologists use this technique to enhance their on-court or on-field performance. Students should use it to improve their in-class concentration, stay on-task, and make their studying more constructive.

Think of a sport you play or another hobby or extracurricular activity.

List 3 things that you can improve upon:

1.

2.

3.

What are the actual steps that you can take to improve these things? Visualize yourself doing them.

For example, if you have trouble shooting in soccer, imagine yourself dribbling down the field, pointing your balancing foot toward the goal, winding up for the shot, striking the ball, and the ball hitting the back of the net.

_____

_____

_____

Think of a subject in school that you struggle with.

List 3 things that you can improve upon:

1.

2.

3.

What are the things that you KNOW you should be doing?
How can you make sure that you do it?

For example, if you know that you never check your work on tests and always make careless mistakes, remember what you're supposed to do and read through your test before turning it in.

_____

_____

_____

Bonus Sections – Helping you Function Beyond Executive Function:

Studying for Tests, Quizzes, and Exams

- Middle school and high school have more frequent and more stressful formative and summative assessments compared to elementary school.

    - Formative assessments are quizzes and graded homework that are usually re-takeable.

    - Summatives count more – they are usually unit tests and not re-takeable.

    - Teachers are required to assign a certain number of formative/summative assessments per quarter.

- The best way to minimize stress for yourself over these assessments is to prepare for them by using the best ways that you can.

- That way, you will be able to answer all the questions with ease and never worry about not knowing the answer or guessing.

Helpful Study Habits

- The tried-and-true Study Sheet:

  - Before a test or quiz, go through your notes and copy down important key words, definitions, equations, or practice problems on a single sheet of paper.

  - Rewriting notes helps you remember the information.

  - Having all the information on a single sheet allows people to have everything they need to know in one place.

Sample Study Sheet

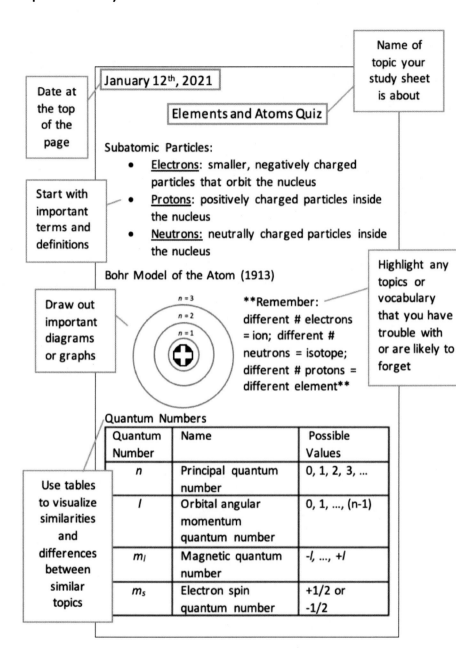

January 12ᵗʰ, 2021

Elements and Atoms Quiz

Subatomic Particles:
- Electrons: smaller, negatively charged particles that orbit the nucleus
- Protons: positively charged particles inside the nucleus
- Neutrons: neutrally charged particles inside the nucleus

Bohr Model of the Atom (1913)

$n = 3$
$n = 2$
$n = 1$

Remember: different # electrons = ion; different # neutrons = isotope; different # protons = different element

Quantum Numbers

Quantum Number	Name	Possible Values
n	Principal quantum number	0, 1, 2, 3, …
l	Orbital angular momentum quantum number	0, 1, …, (n-1)
m_l	Magnetic quantum number	$-l$, …, $+l$
m_s	Electron spin quantum number	+1/2 or -1/2

Date at the top of the page

Name of topic your study sheet is about

Start with important terms and definitions

Draw out important diagrams or graphs

Highlight any topics or vocabulary that you have trouble with or are likely to forget

Use tables to visualize similarities and differences between similar topics

More Study Tips

- Re-read your notes out loud.

- Reach out to your classmates and meet in a study group before a test.

- Don't try to re-learn all the material the night before! You will retain more information if you study a little bit every day.

- Take advantage of your teacher (i.e., the person writing the test!) and ask them clarifying questions.

- Block yourself from using media while studying.

Test-Taking Habits

Even if teachers swear that they don't ask any trick questions, tests can still feel like they do! You've studied as much as you can until this moment, so now it's all about showing what you know and avoiding any dumb mistakes:

Read the directions for each question carefully! Look out for phrases like "all of the following EXCEPT" or "which one is NOT correct"

Know the difference between different verbs they use in questions:

Give an example, describe, compare, show, prove, summarize, etc.

Read all the options before choosing one in multiple choice

If you have time, read over all your answers a second or third time, just to make sure you're answering them correctly. Of course, it's more important that you answer as many questions as you can!

Try to answer a math problem a different way and see if you get the same solution

If you don't understand a question/answer option, ask your teacher. It can't hurt and they'll usually be able to give you a hint toward the answer

Relax, take a deep breath, and trust that you studied the best you could

se your Classmates to your and their Advantage:

- Everyone in your class is in the same boat.

- If you don't understand something, they might not understand it either! They can talk to the teacher with you if you don't want to ask questions alone.

- Reach out to your classmates if you are having trouble with any assignments or the class in general. They might be able to explain things in a way that makes more sense to you!

- Teaching content to someone else helps you understand it better! If you can explain something well to someone else, then you really know you understand it.

- Talking to your classmates helps make friends at your new school.

When You Feel Like You've Messed Up, What Do You Do?

Even when you set yourself up for success by writing everything in your agenda book, you still may forget an assignment because you're human! Note: teachers have heard every excuse before.

- The best way to explain what happened is by being honest with your teachers because they do not want to hear excuses! Btw teachers know when you're lying.

- Teachers are more likely to be understanding and give you a second chance if you're honest with them.

- Taking responsibility for your mistakes and being honest are important life skills that show maturity to your teachers.

Yet More Ways to Get Good Grades:

Engage yourself in classes

Talk to teachers – be proactive and get help

Figure out quickly how and where you learn best

Check grades often and shoot high

Move on if you don't get good grades, don't dwell on it

Good grades depend on how hard you're willing to work for them

Has getting a "bad" grade ever made you feel like this? Put a check in the column that applies to you for each of the feelings after getting a "bad" grade on a test, quiz, or homework. Add in 2-3 other feelings you get after a "bad" grade on a test, quiz or homework.

Feelings after getting a "bad" grade on a test, quiz, or homework	How often do you feel like this from a "bad" grade		
	1 – not at all	2 – somewhat	3 – a lot
This grade means that I'm gonna fail the class			
My teacher hates me or thinks I'm stupid because I got this grade			
My friends are smarter than me because they got a good grade and I didn't			

I'm never going to college because of this grade

What do you do about "bad" grades?

- Forgive yourself.

- Don't be upset at your teacher, accept responsibility.

- It is difficult to see your grades so different from elementary school.

- Don't compare yourself to others! Everyone is different.

- Don't feel like you have to talk to other people about your grades (or feel like you have to ask them about theirs).

- Not cool to compete with your friends about grades.

Whatever happens, cheating is never worth it:

- Getting a low percentage is better than a zero if caught cheating.

- If you or a friend copies each other's homework, the worst-case scenario is that you both get zeroes, or get reported.

- Instead, give your friend alternative ways you can help them with their homework.

- You don't want something like academic dishonesty on your record when you're applying to colleges.

Hint: Don't use services like Chegg that track your activity - you can get caught cheating (for example, if teachers have to check for academic dishonesty, wrong answers might be posted).

Bottom line: If you do everything in this workbook and learn everything you can about doing well in school and in the rest of your life, you'll always have far better means than cheating.

Extra Information on Getting Along Well with Teachers:

 A good relationship with your teachers will make it even easier for them to help you

 All teachers want to see you succeed and they are there to help you! Students who succeed & don't fail make teachers look good; so they truly want you to do well and it's a bonus for them when you do

 Be kind, polite, and set a good example for your classmates by paying attention and doing your homework

 Even strict or "mean" teachers are human beings who appreciate kindness and respect from their students

inal Considerations

eing consistent with the scientist-practitioner model from which his Executive Functioning workbook derives, it is important to ote that research conducted over the past two decades has evealed that good quality student-teacher relationships are ssociated with learning/ educational progress and happiness/ atisfaction in school.

ndings by J. Kim (2020) indicate that positive relationships with eachers had a stronger association with adult mental and hysical health outcomes in some areas than did student-student elationships! Beyond friendship and peer group relationships, herefore, connecting with teachers may bode for better school ears overall.

 closing, try to incorporate and apply as many executive skills as ossible during your days and evenings – whether for school or r other things – and discover which changes you found the ost helpful. We all figure out our own 'tricks' that work too. Feel ee to share those tricks with other people because what works r you might work for them!

Selected References

Ahmed, S. F., Tang, S., Waters, N. E., & Davis-Kean, P. (2019). Executive function and academic achievement: Longitudinal relations from early childhood to adolescence. *Journal of Educational Psychology, 111,* 446-458.

Anthony, C. J. & Ogg, J. (2020). Executive function, learning-related behaviors, and science growth from kindergarten to fourth grade. *Journal of Educational Psychology, 112,* 1563-1581.

Burgess, K. B., Bowker, J. C., Wilson, C. S., Stotsky, M., & Hastings, P. D. (2020, August). Biopsychosocial Health Intervention and Prevention (BHIP) Program: Pilot study shows efficient and effective for adolescents' functioning. *Poster presentation made at the American Psychological Association,* Washington, DC.

Burgess, K. B., Hastings, P. D., & Bowker, J. C. (2019). BHIP takes aim at teenagers' stress, anxiety, executive function, interpersonal skills, and overall mental health: Pilot study shows comprehensive health program significantly improves adolescents' functioning. *Cision.*

Camerota, M., Willoughby, M. T., & Blair, C. B. (2020). Measurement models for studying child executive functioning: Questioning the status quo. *Developmental Psychology, 56,* 2236-2245.

edovic, K., D'Aguiar, C., & Pruessner, J. C. (2009). What stress does to your brain: A review of neuroimaging studies. *The Canadian Journal of Psychiatry*, 54(1), 6-15.

ioia, G. A., Isquith, P. K., Guy, S. C., & Kenworthy, L. (2015). Behavior Rating Inventory of Executive Function ®, Second Edition (BRIEF®2). Lutz, FL: PAR Inc.

rol, M. & De Raedt, R. (2018). The effect of positive mood on flexible processing of affective information. *Emotion, 18,* 819-833.

an, G. H-P., Helm, J., Iucha, C., Hastings, P. D., Zahn-Waxler, C., & Klimes-Dougan, B. (2016). Are executive functioning deficits concurrently and predictively associated with depressive and anxiety symptoms in adolescents? *Journal of Clinical Child and Adolescent Psychology, 45,* 44-58.

im, J. (2020). The quality of social relationships in schools and adult health: Differential effects of student-student versus student-teacher relationships. *Journal of School Psychology*, ISSN: 2578-4218.

add, G. W. & Burgess, K. B. (1999). Charting the relationship trajectories of aggressive, withdrawn, and aggressive/ withdrawn children in early grade school. *Child Development, 70,* 910-929.

ang, J. W. & Kell, H. J. (2020). General mental ability and specific abilities: Their relative importance for extrinsic career success. *Journal of Applied Psychology, 105,* 1047-1061.

Liang, Y., Cao, H., Zhou, N., Li, J., & Zhang, L. (2020). Early home learning environment predicts early adolescents' adjustment through cognitive abilities in middle childhood. *Journal of Family Psychology, 34,* 905-917.

Lister-Landman, K. M., Domoff, S. E., & Dubow, E. F. (2017). The role of compulsive texting in adolescents' academic functioning. *Psychology of Popular Media Culture, 6,* 311-325.

Moffett, L. & Morrison F. J. (2020). Off-task behavior in kindergarten: Relations to executive function and academic achievement. *Journal of Educational Psychology, 112,* 938-955.

Perry, N. B., Dollar, J. M., Calkins, S. D., Keane, S. P., & Shanahan, L. (2018). Childhood self-regulation as a mechanism through which early overcontrolling parenting is associated with adjustment in preadolescence. *Developmental Psychology, 54,* 1542-1554.

Wang, Y. & Hawk, S. T. (2020). Expressive enhancement, suppression, and flexibility in childhood and adolescence: Longitudinal links with peer relations. *Emotion, 20,* 1059-1073.

Made in the USA
Monee, IL
27 August 2021